ínspirations

FRAMES

Over 20 decorative projects for the home

ínspirations

FRAMES

Over 20 decorative projects for the home

VICTORIA BROWN

PHOTOGRAPHY BY GRAHAM RAE

LORENZ BOOKS
LONDON • NEW YORK • SYDNEY • BATH

First published in the UK in 1997 by Lorenz Books

© Anness Publishing Limited 1997

Lorenz Books is an imprint of
Anness Publishing Limited
Hermes House
88–89 Blackfriars Road
London SE1 8HA

This edition distributed in Canada by Raincoast Books,
8680 Cambie Street, Vancouver, British Columbia V6P 6M9

ISBN 1 85967 536 0

A CIP catalogue record for this book is available from the British Library

Publisher: Joanna Lorenz
Project Editor: Sarah Ainley
Designer: Bobbie Colgate Stone
Photographer: Graham Rae
Step Photographer: Rose Jones
Stylist: Leeann Mackenzie

Additional photography pp70–1 by Debbie Patterson

Printed in Hong Kong

1 3 5 7 9 10 8 6 4 2

CONTENTS

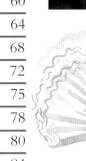

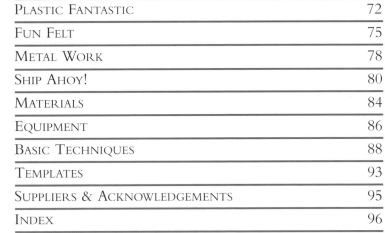

INTRODUCTION	6
SPECIAL EFFECTS	8
GOOD AS GOLD	12
PLASTER CAST	15
CROWN JEWELS	18
DRIFT AWAY	21
SHELL FRAMES	24
STRING SPIRALS	27
PUNCHED TIN	30
MADE TO MEASURE	34
PAPER MAGIC	38
ON THE TILES	42
CUT FLOWERS	45
SEQUINS AND BEADS	48
COUNTRY CROSS STITCH	51
RIBBON WEAVE	54
SWEET HEARTS	57
NATURAL SELECTION	60
ON DISPLAY	64
SUNFLOWER MIRROR	68
PLASTIC FANTASTIC	72
FUN FELT	75
METAL WORK	78
SHIP AHOY!	80
MATERIALS	84
EQUIPMENT	86
BASIC TECHNIQUES	88
TEMPLATES	93
SUPPLIERS & ACKNOWLEDGEMENTS	95
INDEX	96

INTRODUCTION

WHENEVER I VISIT art galleries, my eye is often drawn from the paintings I have come to see to the frames surrounding them. The purpose of a frame may be to offset the work of art held within it, but frames are immensely interesting in their own right, and the style of frames in galleries is often as varied as the paintings. The very best frames are those which not only accentuate the painting but are also beautiful to look at.

I am not suggesting that in this book we will be showing you how to create intricately moulded frames, even though we do show you how to gild a frame. What this book will do is show you a selection of framing styles, from the traditional to the quirky, as a guide to creating, adapting and revamping your own frames. The frames here are not designed to hold works of art; rather they are personal pieces to be filled with family photographs and favourite pictures, to reflect your own style.

With over 20 projects in this book you are sure to find a frame to fit into your home. We have used a wealth of craft techniques, from papier-mâché and cross stitch to casting a frame from plaster. Each project contains clear instructions showing you how each stage should progress, plus there is a comprehensive section on all of the necessary materials, equipment and the basic techniques. I hope this book will inspire you to create eyecatching framed displays throughout your home.

Deborah Barker

SPECIAL EFFECTS

Paint effects on walls are very popular. Here are three small projects for you to practise the art of stamping, distressing and roller painting. Experiment with dark and light coloured paints to create different looks.

YOU WILL NEED

CHECKERED EFFECT
wooden picture frame
paintbrush
wood primer
small foam roller
four rubber bands
wallpaper paste
emulsion (latex) paint in blue
paint tray
cotton buds or cotton balls

STAMPED EFFECT
paintbrush
wooden picture frame
emulsion (latex) paint in dark blue, light
blue and pale yellow
felt-tipped pen
eraser
craft knife
natural sponge
scrap paper
cotton buds or cotton balls

DISTRESSED PAINT EFFECT
paintbrush
wooden picture frame
wood primer
emulsion (latex) paint in green and blue
wax candle
paint scraper

CHECKERED EFFECT

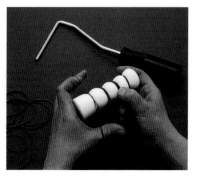

1 Using a paintbrush, prime the wooden picture frame with a base coat of wood primer. Bind the small foam roller at equal distances with four rubber bands and set it aside.

2 Mix up the wallpaper paste to the same consistency as the emulsion (latex) paint. To make the paint translucent, combine equal amounts of the blue emulsion and the prepared wallpaper paste in a paint tray. Load the roller, wiping off any excess paint with a cotton bud or cotton ball.

3 Roll vertical lines of paint on the frame and let dry.

4 Roll horizontal lines on the frame and let dry.

STAMPED EFFECT

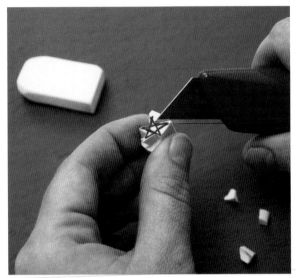

1 Using a brush, paint the frame with a base coat of dark blue emulsion (latex) paint. With a felt-tipped pen, draw a star design on the eraser and cut away the area around the design, using a craft knife.

2 Dip the natural sponge into the light blue emulsion paint and dab on a piece of scrap paper to remove any excess paint. Sponge all over the frame. Let dry.

3 Apply pale yellow emulsion to the rubber stamp with a cotton bud or cotton ball.

4 Use the stamp to print stars at random over the sponged frame.

DISTRESSED PAINT EFFECT

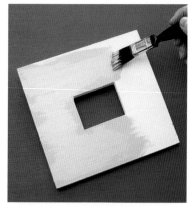

1 Using a paintbrush, prime the frame with a base coat of wood primer. Let dry, then paint with a coat of green emulsion (latex). Allow to dry.

2 Take a wax candle and rub it over all of the edges of the frame and a rub few patches in the middle.

3 Paint over the whole frame with blue emulsion paint. Let the paint dry completely.

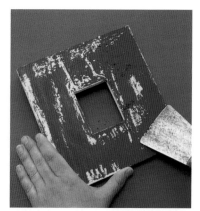

4 Rub over the paint with a paint scraper to reveal the green paint underneath.

GOOD AS GOLD

*Transform a simple wooden frame into a gleaming gilded one with gold leaf,
varnish and acrylic glaze. Gilding is not a quick process but the finished result is
certainly worth the waiting time.*

YOU WILL NEED
wooden picture frame
red oxide spray primer
paintbrush
water-based size
Dutch gold leaf
soft make-up brush
wire (steel) wool
methylated spirits (denatured alcohol)
button polish
old stiff brush
French enamel varnish
rubber gloves
acrylic paint in orange
soft cloth

1 Prime the wooden picture frame with the red oxide spray primer. (Use the spray in a well-ventilated room.)

2 Using a paintbrush, apply a thin but even coat of water-based size, painting over any bubbles that have appeared.

3 Place sheets of gold leaf on the size, dabbing it into place with a soft make-up brush.

4 With wire (steel) wool and methylated spirits (denatured alcohol), rub over the raised areas and a few highlights to reveal some of the base coat.

5 Use a paintbrush to apply a coat of button polish. The polish acts as a sealant on the gold leaf.

6 Dip an old, stiff brush into some French enamel varnish and, wearing gloves, flick back the bristles with your fingers to produce a fine spray of enamel over the frame.

7 Make a glaze of orange acrylic paint, diluting the paint with a little water. Paint the glaze all over the frame.

8 While still wet, wipe off the excess glaze with a soft cloth so that some paint remains in the detail areas. Let dry.

PLASTER CAST

Modelling plaster is readily available and easy to use. Look around for unusual cake tins,
ice cube trays or chocolate moulds for creating plaster shapes. The red plaster frame in this project
has been cleverly tinted using shoe polish as a quick and inexpensive colouring.

YOU WILL NEED
two-part ring cake tin (pan)
petroleum jelly
modelling plaster
bowl
jug (optional)
flexible plastic ice cube tray
nylon scouring pad
soft cloth
coloured shoe polish
wooden frame
paintbrush
white emulsion (latex) paint
strong glue
brush for glue

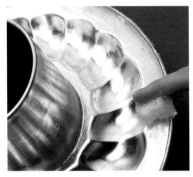

1 Grease the inside of the cake tin (pan) with petroleum jelly. Make sure the tin is assembled and watertight before mixing up the modelling plaster.

2 Mix the plaster by adding modelling plaster to a bowl of water until a mound of plaster forms out of the water. Mix the plaster with your hand.

3 When thoroughly mixed, pour the plaster into the cake tin mould. (You may find it easier to use a jug.) When the mould is half filled, pour the excess plaster into an ice cube tray. Tap the mould to remove any air bubbles from the bottom and the sides.

4 After about 4 or 5 minutes, when the plaster begins to harden, make an indentation in the back of the frame to make a rebate and then throw away this bit of the plaster.

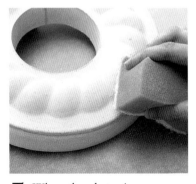

5 When the plaster is completely hard, remove it from the mould and smooth off the sides and any rough edges with a nylon scouring pad.

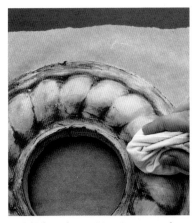

6 Allow the plaster to dry thoroughly – this can take up to a week. With a soft cloth, apply a liberal coating of coloured shoe polish to colour and seal the plaster.

7 After about 10 minutes, rub off the shoe polish with the soft cloth to create highlights on the coloured plaster.

8 To decorate a wooden frame, turn out the plaster shapes from the ice cube tray and smooth off the edges of the bases with the nylon scouring pad.

9 Paint a wooden frame with white emulsion (latex) paint. When the paint is dry, glue on the plaster shapes. Allow the glue to dry completely.

Above: An additional frame decorated with plaster shapes provides variation and makes an effective complement to the main plasterwork frame.

CROWN JEWELS

This papier-mâché frame takes on a new sophistication with the addition of silver paint and foil-wrapped "jewels". You can make the frame as simple or as lavish as you wish by your choice of paint colours and accessories.

YOU WILL NEED
tracing paper
soft pencil
corrugated cardboard
scissors
cardboard
PVA (white) glue
brush for gluing
bowl
newspaper
tissue paper
white acrylic primer
paintbrushes
acrylic paints in purple and green
poster paint in silver
assorted costume "jewels"
tin foil
tape

1 Trace the template at the back of the book and enlarge if necessary. Cut out two corrugated cardboard frames. Cut out three squares or triangles of plain cardboard for each of the four sides of the frame.

2 Using PVA (white) glue attach a stack of three cardboard shapes to each side of the back of one frame. Place the second card frame on top of the shapes and glue it in position.

3 Dilute the PVA, two parts glue to one part water, in a bowl. Tear off strips of newspaper and dip in the diluted glue. Start by laying paper strips over the gaps at the sides of the frame.

4 Build up the papier-mâché in layers all over the frame, painting the diluted glue on to the papier-mâché and covering with dry strips of paper. Build up about six layers in this way.

5 Make two borders with tissue paper soaked in diluted glue and twisted into ropes. Lay one rope around the outer edge and one around the inner edge of the frame. Let dry.

▶

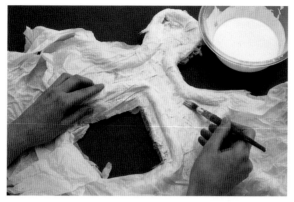

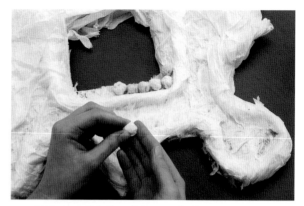

6 Next, cover the whole frame with two sheets of tissue paper laid down individually and soaked with the diluted glue.

7 Make small balls of glue-soaked tissue paper and glue around the inside of the frame. Allow to dry thoroughly – this may take several days.

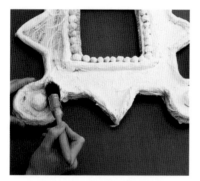

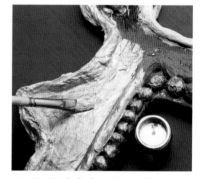

8 Prime the frame all over with several coats of white acrylic primer.

9 Paint the frame with a base coat of acrylic paints in purple and green.

10 Lightly brush on silver poster paint, letting the base colours show through.

11 Wrap the edges of the "jewels" with tin foil torn into small squares.

12 Dull the foil with a little of the purple acrylic paint.

13 Glue the jewels on to the frame. Tape your picture to the back of the frame.

DRIFT AWAY

Good, clean driftwood is hard to find even if you live near the sea, but you can make your own "driftwood" from old wooden boards or packing cases. Break the wood into pieces and distress it with a chisel to add authenticity.

YOU WILL NEED
packing crate or wooden board
wood chisel
hammer
surform
coarse sandpaper
watercolour paints in green, crimson and blue
paintbrush
two-part epoxy resin glue
hardboard
junior hacksaw
blackboard paint
drill
1 m/1⅛ yd thin sisal string
1 m/1⅛ yd thick sisal rope

1 Break the wood into smaller lengths and split it, using a chisel and a hammer.

2 Break the wood into four lengths for the sides of the frame. Gouge out chunks from the sides of the wood to make it look more weatherbeaten.

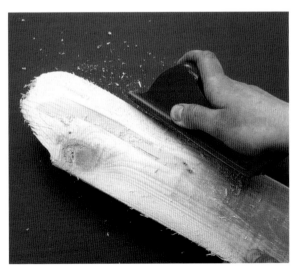

3 Use a surform to file the edges until they are smooth.

4 Sand down with coarse sandpaper to remove any splinters, and round off the edges.

5 Combine a thin colourwash using green, crimson and blue watercolour paints and brush it on to the wood. Let dry.

6 Using the two-part epoxy resin glue, glue the frame together. Let dry. Use the hacksaw to cut a piece of hardboard to size and paint the smooth surface with blackboard paint.

7 Tape the blackboard to the back of the frame and drill four holes, one in each corner. At each of the bottom corners, thread sisal string from front to back on the left-hand side, across the back of the frame, and out to the front through the right-hand hole. Tie the ends in knots on the front of the frame.

8 Enlarge the two holes at the top of the frame and pass the thick sisal rope through the holes as before, leaving enough excess rope to hang the frame. Tie the ends in knots on the front.

SHELL FRAMES

Here are two perfect projects for displaying all those shells so carefully collected on holiday. You only need a few to create an impact. Bags of shells are also available in craft and gift stores or you may be able to get scallop shells from a local fishmonger.

YOU WILL NEED

NATURAL FRAME
emulsion (latex) paint
PVA (white) glue
paintbrush
wooden frame
dish cloth
shells
strong glue

GOLD FRAME
wooden frame
gold spray paint
shells
scrap paper
strong glue
china marker

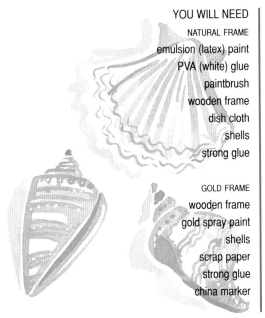

NATURAL FRAME

1 Dilute the emulsion (latex) paint with water and add 15 ml/1 tbsp PVA (white) glue. Brush the colourwash over the frame and, as you apply it, rub off the excess with a dish cloth.

2 Use the colourwash to colour the shells. Allow the painted shells to dry completely.

3 When the shells are completely dry, arrange and glue them on to the frame with strong glue.

GOLD FRAME

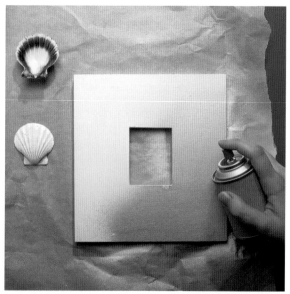

1 In a well-ventilated area, spray the wooden frame with the gold paint. Let dry.

2 Spread the shells on some scrap paper and spray them evenly with the gold paint. Let dry.

Above: Spray-painting all of the shells in a single colour will give the frame a strong contemporary look.

3 Arrange and glue the shells with strong glue to the frame. Mark their positions first with a china marker, as each shell is slightly different and will have its own place.

STRING SPIRALS

Even a humble ball of string can be utilized decoratively. These two frames use sisal and cotton string to create loops and spirals. Leave the string in its natural state or finish it with a coat of paint to tie in with your colour scheme.

YOU WILL NEED

RECTANGULAR FRAME

paper & pen

scissors

corrugated cardboard

sisal string

PVA (white) glue

craft knife

emulsion (latex) paint in matt white

paintbrush

CIRCULAR FRAME

wooden frame

pen

PVA (white) glue

cotton string

emulsion (latex) paint in blue

paintbrush

RECTANGULAR FRAME

1 Draw 5 cm/2 in diameter circles on paper and cut out to use as templates. Draw around the circles on the corrugated cardboard to make a frame shape.

2 Starting in the middle of the circles and working out, glue on sisal string in spirals. Fill in each of the circles in this way.

3 At the corners of the frame, fill in the spaces with smaller spirals of string.

4 When the glue is completely dry, cut around the edge of the frame with a craft knife.

5 Glue two lengths of sisal string over the cut edge of the cardboard to neaten the edge.

▶

6 Paint the front of the frame with a coat of matt white emulsion (latex) paint.

7 Make a back and stand for the back of the frame out of corrugated cardboard. Paint the stand and the back of the frame with matt white emulsion paint. When the paint is dry, glue the stand in position.

1 As a simple variation, use cotton string to decorate a wooden frame. Draw an outline on the frame and glue the string along the outline. Add two more pieces of string following the first outline.

Above: The flexiblity of string makes it an excellent choice of material for decorating frames: almost any design can be successfully achieved.

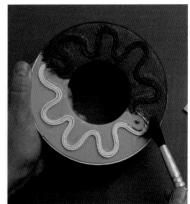

2 Glue cotton string around the edge of the frame. When the glue is dry, paint both the frame and the stand with blue emulsion (latex) paint.

PUNCHED TIN

Tin is a soft metal that can be decorated easily using a centre punch or a blunt chisel to create dots and lines. Keep your punched design simple and graphic as too much fine detail will get lost when the design is punched out.

YOU WILL NEED

wooden frame
cardboard
felt-tipped pen
scissors
tape
sheet of tin
centre punch
hammer
tin snips
protective gloves (optional)
chisel
ridged paint scraper
copper nails
paper towels & salt water (optional)
wax & paintbrush (optional)
metal polish & soft cloth (optional)
clear varnish (optional)

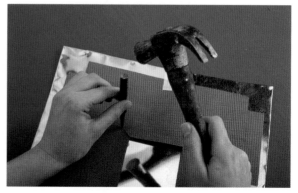

1 Lay the wooden frame on a piece of cardboard and draw around the outline with a felt-tipped pen. Add extra length at the outside edges and around the centre to allow for turnings, and cut out the template with scissors. Tape the cardboard template on to a sheet of tin. Mark the corners using a centre punch and hammer, and mark the straight lines with a felt-tipped pen.

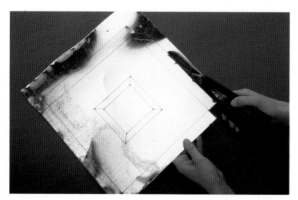

2 Cut out the shape with tin snips. (You may want to wear protective gloves to protect your hands from the sharp edges of the tin.)

3 Using a hammer and chisel, cut through the centre of the frame in a diagonal line then use tin snips to cut out the remaining sides and open it out to a square.

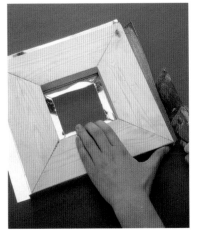

4 Lay the wooden frame on the tin and use a ridged paint scraper to coax the metal up the sides of the frame.

5 Turn over the frame and push down the metal edges in the centre, again using the ridged paint scraper.

6 Cut two strips of tin, each 20 x 2 cm/8 x ¾ in. Snip at the halfway mark and fold at a 90° angle. Nail the strips to the inner edge of the frame, using copper nails.

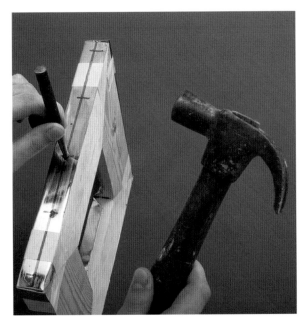

7 Carefully hammer copper nails along the outer edges of the frame so that the tin is firmly secured in place.

8 Draw a freehand feather design on the tin frame. Using a felt-tipped pen to draw the design means that any errors can be easily wiped away.

▶

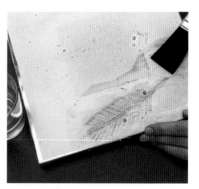

9 Press the feather design onto the tin in dots, using a hammer and centre punch.

10 Alternatively, use a blunt chisel and a hammer to press the design on to the tin in straight lines.

11 There are two ways to finish the frame. To rust the tin, cover it with a paper towel and dampen with salt water. Keep the paper damp until the frame has rusted – this will take 2–7 days, depending on how much salt is used. Remove the paper, leave the frame to dry and seal the rust with a coat of wax.

12 Alternatively, clean the tin with metal polish and a soft cloth, removing any traces of marker pen. To preserve the finish, seal with a clear varnish.

Above: The dramatic effect of a rusted finish sits equally well alongside any style of interior, from contemporary to traditional country.

MADE TO MEASURE

*Hardware stores stock mouldings in different styles, ranging from plain and simple
to carved and richly ornate. Combine two or three mouldings to make
your own made-to-measure frame.*

YOU WILL NEED

BLACK FRAME
tenon saw
1.6 m/64 in barley twist moulding
80 cm/32 in semi-circular moulding
80 cm/32 in flat moulding
wood glue
mitre block
black wood stain or ink
paintbrush
black shoe polish
soft cloth
shoe brush

NATURAL FRAME
tenon saw
80 cm/32 in of 5 mm/¼ in square moulding
80 cm/32 in of 1.5 x 2 cm/⅝ x ¾ in flat
moulding
wood glue
2.4 m/2⅝ yd decorative moulding
mitre block
tenon saw
corner clamp
clear polyurethane varnish
brush for varnish

BLACK FRAME

1 Using a tenon saw, cut four 20 cm/8 in lengths
from each moulding. Using wood glue, join a
barley twist and a semi-circular moulding strip to
either side of the flat moulding. (The semi-circular
moulding will form the rebate of the frame.) Allow
the glue to dry completely.

2 Mitre the lengths of assembled moulding using
a mitre block and tenon saw, and make up the
frame (see Basic Techniques). Mitre the barley twist
moulding and glue to the front of the frame. Let the
glue dry completely.

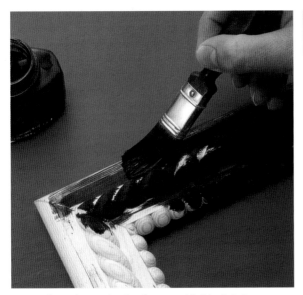

3 When dry, stain the frame with black ink or wood stain applied with a paintbrush.

4 After a couple of hours, when the stain is dry, seal the wood and add a sheen with black shoe polish, applied with a soft cloth. Buff it up with a shoe brush.

NATURAL FRAME

1 Using a tenon saw, cut four 20 cm/8 in lengths of square moulding. Cut four pieces of flat moulding to the same length. Glue a piece of square moulding to the edge of each piece of flat moulding.

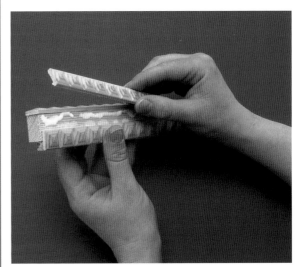

2 Cut 12 pieces of decorative moulding, each 20 cm/8 in long. Glue two decorative mouldings to the front surface and one on the side. Let the glue dry thoroughly.

▶

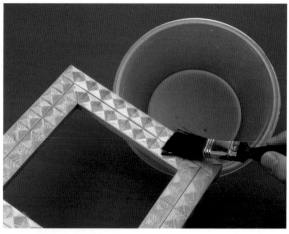

3 Carefully mitre the ends of the assembled wood, using a mitre block and tenon saw, and glue and clamp the corners together (see Basic Techniques).

4 Apply a coat of clear polyurethane varnish to seal the wood and enhance the natural colours and grain of the wood.

Left: Wooden decorative mouldings give the frame a highly professional finish.

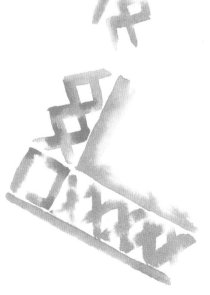

PAPER MAGIC

Paper and cardboard are readily available and easy to use for making frames. Layers of cardboard glued together produce a wonderful three-dimensional effect. For best results, make sure the cardboard is accurately and squarely cut, and that all the edges are aligned.

YOU WILL NEED

CLASSICAL COLUMNS
tracing paper & pencil
mounting board
cutting mat
45° mat cutter
craft knife & metal ruler
rubber solution adhesive
double-sided tape or glue

PUNCHED PAPER
5 mm/¼ in thick polyboard
pencil
craft knife
cutting mat
thick watercolour paper
glue
towel or cloth
darning needle

CLASSICAL COLUMNS

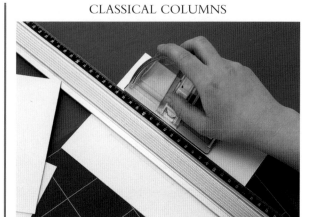

1 Trace the templates at the back of the book and enlarge if necessary. Cut out the basic frame shape from mounting board, using a cutting mat and a 45° mat cutter (see Equipment).

2 Using a craft knife, cut four strips for each column and the steps, and four triangles for the roof, from another piece of mounting board.

3 Glue down the steps with rubber solution adhesive (any excess can be rubbed off when dry). Line up the cardboard strips with the frame base.

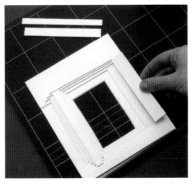

4 Next, glue the roof in place with the rubber solution adhesive. Let dry.

5 Then glue on the two columns, cutting the length of the strips to fit if necessary.

6 Finally, insert your picture using double-sided tape or glue and attach a piece of mounting board to the back as a stand.

PUNCHED PAPER

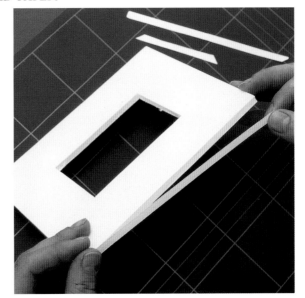

1 Draw the basic frame shape on the polyboard and cut out, using a craft knife and cutting mat.

2 Cut 5 mm/¼ in wide strips of watercolour paper and glue to the inside and outside edges of the frame. Let the glue dry completely.

3 Cut out a piece of watercolour paper to the same size as the frame front and, using the template at the back of the book, draw the design on the back.

4 Lay the paper on a towel or cloth and, following the design, pierce a line of dots through the drawing with a darning needle.

5 When finished, glue the pierced paper to the front of the frame.

6 Make a simple stand from polyboard and attach it to the back of the frame with glue.

ON THE TILES

Small mosaic tiles make an attractive Mediterranean-style frame that would be perfect in a conservatory or bathroom. Plan the dimensions of the frame to suit the size of tiles, to avoid having to cut and fit odd-shaped pieces.

YOU WILL NEED
pencil & metal ruler
18 mm/¾ in thick medium-density fibreboard (MDF)
saw
drill
jigsaw
wood glue
white acrylic primer
paintbrush
tile cement
tooth-edged adhesive spreader
glass mosaic tiles
grout
soft cloth
mirror
narrow picture moulding
two ring screws
brass picture wire

1 Draw a frame on medium-density fibreboard (MDF). Cut out using a saw. Drill corner holes for the centre and cut out with a jigsaw. Cut out a shelf and glue to the frame with wood glue. Let dry.

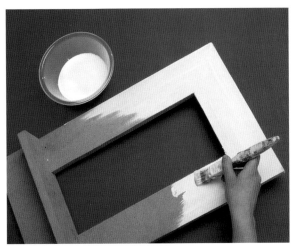

2 Prime both sides of the frame and shelf with white acrylic primer to seal it.

3 Apply tile cement to a small area, using a fine tooth-edged adhesive spreader.

4 Apply a random selection of tiles, leaving a 2 mm/1⁄16 in gap between each tile. Continue over the rest of the frame, working on a small area at a time. Tile the edges with a single row of tiles.

5 Following the manufacturer's instructions, let the tile cement dry for a couple of hours. Next, spread grout in between the tiles, scraping off the excess.

6 Clean off any remaining grout with a soft cloth. Let the grout dry thoroughly.

7 Lay a mirror face down on the back of the frame and secure it with narrow picture moulding, glued in place with wood glue. Let dry.

8 Finally, screw two ring screws in place on the back of the mirror, and tie on picture wire to hang the frame.

CUT FLOWERS

The craft of decoupage originated in the 18th century and comes from the French word "découper" meaning "to cut out". This project uses photocopied images cut out and coloured with watercolour paints but you can use ready-coloured scraps to save time.

YOU WILL NEED
brown paper
pen & ruler
scissors
6 mm/¼ in medium-density fibreboard
(MDF), three pieces cut to
20 x 22 cm/8 x 8½ in
drill
jigsaw
medium and large-sized surforms
wood glue
sandpaper
white acrylic primer
paintbrushes
white emulsion (latex) paint
selection of photocopied pictures
small, sharp scissors
watercolour paints
glue stick
gloss varnish
brush for varnish

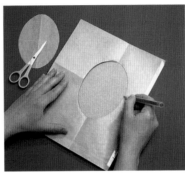

1 Cut a piece of brown paper 20 x 22 cm/8 x 8½ in and fold it in quarters. Draw a shape in the middle for the frame opening and cut out. Open out the template and mark out the oval on one piece of medium-density fibreboard (MDF).

2 From the other two pieces of MDF, cut out a rectangle, 11.5 x 15 cm/4½ x 6 in, to fit over the oval. Drill a hole in the corners of the rectangle and use a jigsaw to cut out the shape.

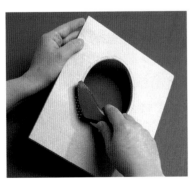

3 With a medium surform, file down the edge of the opening to soften the curve.

4 Glue the three pieces of MDF together with wood glue and let dry.

5 Use a large and a medium-sized surform to smooth the frame and to round the edges. ▶

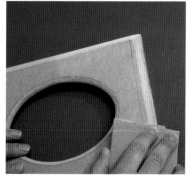

6 Finish all the edges with sandpaper to make them extra smooth.

7 Prime the frame with white acrylic primer and then apply a coat of emulsion (latex) paint.

8 Cut out a selection of photo-copied images using small, sharp scissors. Tint the cut-outs with watercolour paints.

Above: The beauty of decoupage is that whichever style of decoration you choose, it is always easily – and instantly – achievable.

9 Glue the cut-outs on to the frame using a glue stick.

10 Varnish the frame to seal the images and to give the frame a glossy finish.

SEQUINS AND BEADS

This delicate and nostalgic frame encrusted with beads will suit a special family photograph and become a family heirloom. The ribbon is folded back to reveal the velvet and satin sides as a background for the beads.

YOU WILL NEED
pencil
metal ruler
mounting board
cutting mat
craft knife
white calico
scissors
needle
matching embroidery threads (floss)
6 cm/2½ in-wide satin-backed velvet ribbon
15 mm/⅝ in-wide green ribbon
small gold glass beads
translucent sequins
clear crystals

1 Draw out the shape of the frame on mounting board. The frame pictured measured 18 x 13 cm/7 x 5 in with 4 cm/ 1½ in-wide borders.

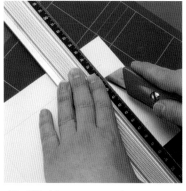

2 Working on a cutting mat, cut out the frame, using a metal ruler and craft knife.

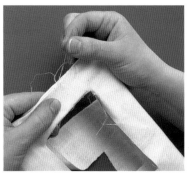

3 Cover the back and front of the frame with white calico, oversewing the edges and turning under the raw edges as you go.

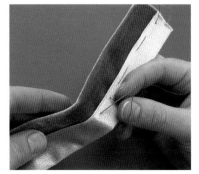

4 Measure around the four sides of the frame and cut a piece of satin-backed ribbon slightly longer than this measurement. Fold the ribbon so it is the same width as the sides of the frame, and tack down the satin edge.

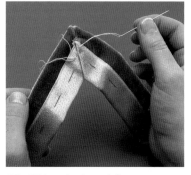

5 Using the board frame as a guide, fold and mitre the corners of the ribbon, tucking under the raw ends to neaten.

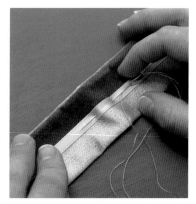

6 Neatly stitch the narrow green ribbon over the seam, using a matching thread colour.

7 Thread four or five small gold glass beads on to a needle and stitch down vertically over the green ribbon. Keeping the beading dense, continue to stitch the beads in place so that the green ribbon is barely seen. Neatly stitch the ribbon frame to the calico-covered frame.

8 Stitch a random selection of translucent sequins and glass beads over the velvet border.

9 Sew clear crystals and small glass beads on to the grey satin part of the ribbon.

10 Stitch a strip of the wider ribbon to the back to hold the photograph. Leave the top edge unstitched so that the photograph can be changed.

COUNTRY CROSS STITCH

Arrange herbs or messages on this simple country cross stitch pinboard made from a napkin or dish towel. The dried herbs can be used for cooking. The woven stripes and uneven weave of the fabric give the frame a natural homely look.

YOU WILL NEED

two dish towels or napkins
small embroidery hoop
red cotton embroidery thread
needle
pins
woven tape
scissors
softboard
junior hacksaw
white cotton thread
herbs and chillies
painted wooden dowel
two cup hooks

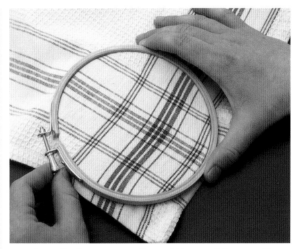

1 Stretch the corner of one dish towel in a small embroidery hoop.

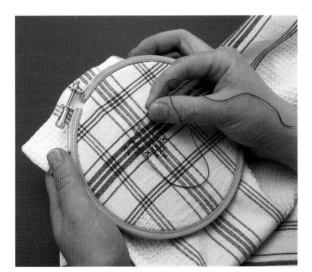

2 Sew a red cross stitch heart in the centre, following the chart at the back of the book. Repeat at each corner of the dish towel.

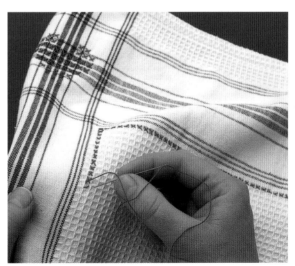

3 Sew a border of cross stitch in the same red thread, where the waffle weave meets the striped edge of the dish towel.

4 With wrong sides facing, pin the two dish towels together. Oversew three edges together, leaving the top edge open.

5 Cut three pieces of woven tape, 20 cm/8 in long, fold them in half and stitch to the inside open edge of one towel.

6 Cut a piece of softboard to the size of the pocket and slide it in through the top edge.

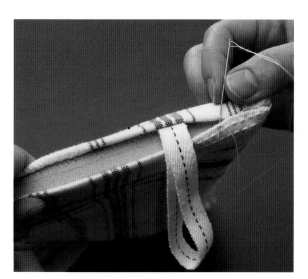

7 Oversew the top edges of the dish towels together, using white cotton thread.

8 Pin the herbs and chillies to the front to make a decorative display. To hang up the frame, insert a painted dowel through the loops and slot into two cup hooks attached to the wall.

RIBBON WEAVE

Take three or four colourful ribbons and weave them into a vivid fabric. Take your time
with the weaving, making sure the ribbons are taut and square to the frame.
Using a glue gun is the easiest way to work, as the glue dries quickly.

YOU WILL NEED
3 m/3½ yd each of 5 mm/¼in-wide
ribbon in four colours
scissors
40 x 30 cm/16 x 12 in frame with
3 cm/1½ in-wide border
glue gun
masking tape
1.5 m/1⅝ yd of 25 mm/1 in-wide
grosgrain ribbon in white

1 Cut the narrow ribbon to length, using the
scissors, allowing an extra 3–4 cm/1¼–1½ in to
wrap around to the back of the frame.

2 On the top right-hand corner of the back of
the frame, glue down the first row of six ribbons,
using a glue gun.

3 Glue down the next six ribbons at right angles to
the first row, keeping the same colour sequence.

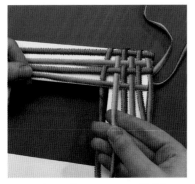

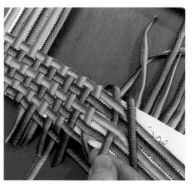

4 Weave the two sets of ribbon together by taking the ribbon under and over in sequence.

5 Hold down the woven ribbon on the back of the frame with masking tape. Start to glue the shorter ribbons on to the frame rebate to make up the bands for the sides.

6 Turn the frame over and weave in the ribbons.

7 When the side weaving is complete, make sure the short ribbons are straight and parallel and glue them in place on the back.

8 Neaten-up the back by gluing white grosgrain ribbon over the cut edges of the ribbon.

SWEET HEARTS

These frames are made from pulped sugar paper, which is moulded into shape,
then dried to make a surprisingly strong material. You can use coloured paper, as here,
or make it in white paper, ready to paint or decorate.

YOU WILL NEED
A2 sheet of coloured sugar paper for each heart
glass bowl
liquidizer (optional)
small heart-shaped cake tin (pan)
tin foil
two bottle caps
paper ribbon
glue
brush
sticky tape
picture

1 For each heart tear the coloured sugar paper into small pieces and place in a bowl. Pour on boiling water and let cool. When it is cool, break it up with your hands or put in a liquidizer. When the paper has broken down into pulp, drain off the excess water.

2 Small cake tins (pans) make suitable moulds for the pulp hearts. Line each cake tin with tin foil to prevent it from rusting.

3 Place a small bottle cap in the centre of the tin mould and pack pulped paper around it. Press out as much water as possible, and continue to pack in more of the pulp.

4 When the pulp is level with the top of the cap, put a larger cap centrally on top to make the rebate to the frame. Pack more pulp around the cap to the top of the tin, draining off the excess water.

5 Lift the foil and the pulp out of the mould and carefully remove the foil. Let the pulp dry in a warm place for 2–3 days. (You can put it in a warm oven to speed up the drying process.) Carefully remove the bottle caps.

6 Glue a loop of paper ribbon to the back of each frame for hanging. Tape a picture into the rebate.

NATURAL SELECTION

Dried poppy seedheads and a selection of twigs are all that are needed to decorate these simple frames. The brown paper tape background echoes the natural colours and textures of the materials.

YOU WILL NEED

FOR EACH FRAME
glue
brown paper
wooden frame
craft knife
paintbrush

POPPIES AND TWIGS
emulsion (latex) paint
PVA (white) glue
soft cloth
twigs
poppy heads
clear glue

STICKS
brown watercolour paint
lichen-covered twigs
multi-purpose glue

POPPY HEADS
brown paper tape
brown watercolour paint
dried poppy heads

POPPIES AND TWIGS

1 Glue torn strips of brown paper around the front edges of the wooden frame.

2 Dilute the emulsion (latex) paint and add 5 ml/ 1 tsp PVA (white) glue. Paint a thin colourwash over the frame.

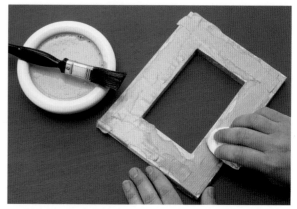

3 Before the wash dries, wipe it off with a soft cloth to leave a very thin coat. Let it soak into the edges of the torn paper.

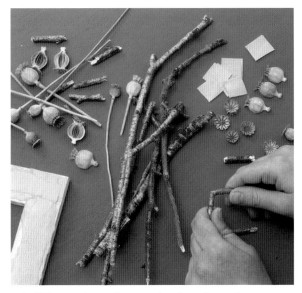

4 Select twigs and poppy heads and cut them to size. Cut through the poppies with a craft knife.

5 Plan your design first, then use clear glue to stick each piece in position on the frame.

STICKS

1 Glue torn strips of brown paper around the front edges of the wooden frame. Paint over the frame with diluted watercolour paint.

2 Stick lichen-covered twigs around the frame using a multi-purpose glue.

61

POPPY HEADS

1 Cover the wooden frame with strips of brown paper tape.

2 Next, glue rough strips of torn brown paper on to the frame.

3 Add pattern and interest to the brown paper with watercolour paint brushed on in fine cross-hatched lines.

4 Cut off the top of the dried poppy heads with a craft knife and glue them on to the frame.

ON DISPLAY

A deep-sided, sectioned frame is the perfect way to display a collection of small objects such as ornaments, jewellery or badges. First plan the frame on paper so you can custom build the sections to suit the size of your collection.

YOU WILL NEED
pencil & metal ruler
length of 30 x 5 mm/1¼ x ¼ in batten
junior hacksaw
wood glue
panel pins (tacks)
hammer
hardboard
white acrylic primer
paintbrush
length of 30 x 2 mm/1¼ x ¹⁄₁₆ in batten
masking tape
PVA (white) glue
tissue paper in assorted colours
acrylic paint in yellow, dark blue and light blue
Indian shisha mirrors

1 Make a rectangular frame with the thicker battening by gluing it with wood glue and securing it using panel pins (tacks).

2 Glue and pin a piece of hardboard to the back. Coat the smooth front side with acrylic primer.

3 Measure and draw out the size of the compartments. Using the thinner battening, cut them out with a junior hacksaw.

4 Put the compartments together with wood glue, taping them with masking tape until they are dry.

5 Coat the wood with PVA (white) glue and cover with torn pieces of coloured tissue paper.

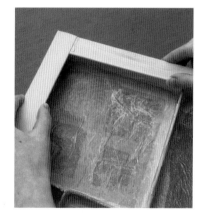

6 Work the tissue paper into the corners and keep applying the glue as necessary. Use lighter colours over stronger colours to create depth of colour.

7 Touch up any areas that need more colour with the yellow acrylic paint.

8 Glue the thinner battening to the outer edge of the frame, using wood glue.

9 Cover the edge of the frame with a collage of tissue paper glued on with PVA.

10 Using a paintbrush, lightly brush over the tissue paper with blue acrylic paint.

11 Glue on small Indian shisha mirrors all around the frame edge.

12 Arrange your collection in the compartments, securing the pieces with glue or a re-usable adhesive, as preferred.

SUNFLOWER MIRROR

You may not always feel cheerful when you look in the mirror, but this sunflower face is sure to lift your spirits. It could grace a dressing table or look good as a decorative object in any room in the house.

YOU WILL NEED
pair of compasses (compass)
pencil
metal ruler
cardboard
craft knife
cutting mat
modelling clay
rolling pin
modelling tools
small terracotta or plastic flowerpot
plaster of Paris, ready mixed
20 cm/8 in of 8mm/⅛ in diameter aluminium tubing
7 cm/2¾ in diameter round mirror
old ball-point pen
acrylic paints in yellow, white, chocolate-brown, green
paint palette
paintbrushes

1 Draw a 12 cm/4¾ in diameter circle on the cardboard and cut it out to make a template. Draw a 6 cm/2½ in diameter circle in the centre and cut out with the craft knife. Roll out the clay to 5 mm /¼ in thick and use the template to cut out two rings.

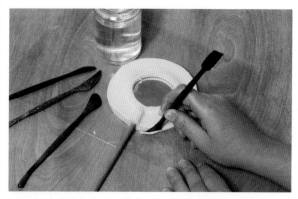

2 Seal the drainage holes in the bottom of the pot with clay. Pour the plaster into the pot. When semi-dry, insert the tube. Let dry. Remove the tube. Place the mirror in the centre of one ring, and place the tube with one end resting on the edge of the circle. Put the second ring on top and seal the edges.

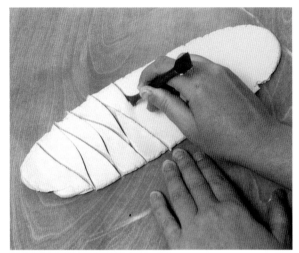

3 Roll out another sheet of clay 3 mm/⅛ in thick, in a long oval shape. Cut out regular flower-petal shapes, using a modelling tool. (You can lightly mark the freehand petal shapes on the clay in pencil, if you find it easier to follow an outline when cutting.)

4 Attach petals all around the back of the mirror, sealing the edges with a modelling tool. Then attach petals to the front of the flower, so they cover the spaces between the back petals. Bend some of the petals to make the sunflower more realistic.

5 Roll two long thin "sausages" of clay and flatten them. Put one on top of the join between the petals and the mirror and one at the edge of the mirror. Press the end of an old pen into the "sausages", to create little depressions all over.

6 Mix the yellow and white paints together in the palette to create a sunny yellow. Paint the sunflower petals in one or two coats of yellow. Let the paint dry thoroughly.

7 Remove the tube from the mirror before
painting. Paint the border around the mirror
with the chocolate-brown paint. Paint the tube in
green. Let the paint dry completely. Reinsert the
tube in the flowerpot and fit the mirror on top.

PLASTIC FANTASTIC

We are surrounded by brightly coloured plastic containers but, as they hold household cleaners and everyday products, we do not see the rainbow in front of us; yet this is a wonderful free source of creative material.

YOU WILL NEED
laundry basket
junior hacksaw
pair of compasses (compass)
craft knife
plastic bottles, lids & caps
pencil
scissors
glue gun

1 Cut off the base of a laundry basket using a junior hacksaw.

2 With a pair of compasses (compass), draw a circle in the middle of the base and cut it out with a craft knife.

3 Wash and clean the plastic bottles, lids and caps. Cut the sides and open out the bottles into flat sheets.

4 Draw freehand flower and leaf shapes on to the plastic and cut out the shapes, using a pair of sharp scissors.

5 Use the craft knife to cut two lines down the middle of each leaf, and lift up the section to make a ridge.

6 Glue the plastic leaves and flowers to the frame, using a glue gun.

7 Glue a bottle cap to the back of the frame, using the glue gun. You can slip the cap over a screw in the wall to hang up the frame.

FUN FELT

*Felt is easy to use because it has plenty of body and doesn't fray,
and felt squares come in a wide array of bright colours. Combine two or three
coloured felts to make a simple mirror frame to hang on the wall.*

YOU WILL NEED
iron
fusible bonding web
felt squares, two lilac and one each
in orange and lime
pencil or felt-tipped pen
sharp scissors
small mirror
craft knife
needle
matching embroidery threads (floss)

1 Iron the fusible bonding web to the orange, lime
and one lilac felt square. Draw a freehand flower
outline on to the backing paper of the bonding web.

2 Cut out the three felt flower shapes with sharp
scissors. Remove the backing paper from the
lilac flower and bond it to the other lilac square.
Cut around the outline to make a double layer flower.

3 Peel the backing paper off the lime flower and
position it on the lilac flower. Use the iron to
fuse the lime flower on top of the lilac flower.

4 Leaving a circle of bonding web paper on the back of the orange flower, draw on a smaller circle, slightly smaller than the mirror, and cut out.

5 Make a small cut across the centre of the lime green felt, through all three layers of felt. Fuse the orange flower on top of the lime flower.

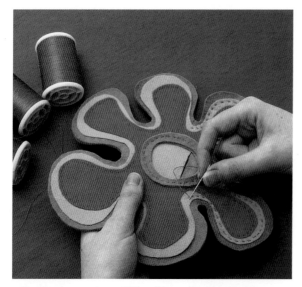

6 Cut out a ring of lilac felt to fit around the centre opening. Stitch in place using simple running stitch in a contrasting colour. Then work running stitches around the edge of the flowers in a contrasting coloured thread. Insert the mirror through the slit in the back of the frame. Make a small loop in buttonhole stitch to hang the frame.

METAL WORK

This frame has been cleverly made from a recycled olive oil can, using the inside and outside to provide the silver and coloured sides. Wear protective gloves to avoid cutting your fingers when handling the tin.

YOU WILL NEED
tin snips
large olive oil can
pencil
paper
pine frame
felt-tipped pen
ridged paint scraper
drill
pop rivet gun and large and small rivets
hammer

1 Using tin snips, open out the can into a large sheet. With a pencil and paper, make a template of each side of the frame, adding overlaps for the inside and outside edges. Use a felt-tipped pen to draw around the template on to the tin. Cut out four pieces of tin.

2 Using a ridged paint scraper, fold one piece of tin around the frame, using stroking motions to burnish the metal and fold it around the frame. When all four sides are covered in the metal, drill through the tin and wood as guide holes for the rivets.

3 Use a pop rivet gun to squeeze in the large rivets to secure the tin to the wood.

4 Cut out coloured triangles from the printed can using tin snips. Hammer each shape on a flat metal surface to flatten it down.

5 Drill guide holes through the centre of each shape into the tin and wood. Insert a rivet into each hole.

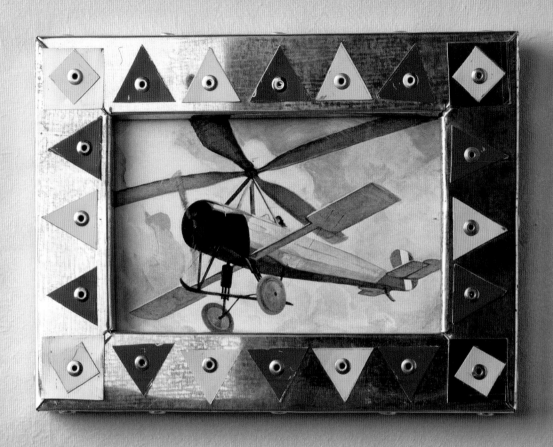

SHIP AHOY!

Children usually enjoy having their photograph taken, and they'll love this colourful novelty frame for displaying their portraits. Why not make a whole fleet of ships for showing off your family photographs?

YOU WILL NEED
tracing paper
soft pencil
cardboard or paper
medium-density fibreboard (MDF)
wood glue
heavy weight
drill
jigsaw
surform
fine sandpaper
white acrylic primer
medium and watercolour paintbrushes
wooden dowel
acrylic paints in red, blue, yellow, white and black
small round white stickers

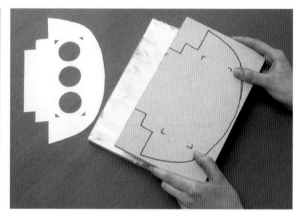

1 Trace the template at the back of the book and enlarge if necessary. Transfer the outline on to cardboard or paper and draw around the shape on to a piece of medium-density fibreboard (MDF). Using wood glue, stick the MDF to another piece of the same size. Let dry under a heavy weight.

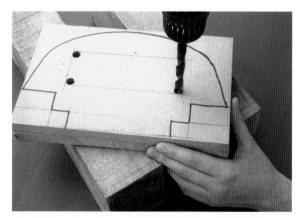

2 When the glue has dried, drill through both pieces of MDF with a large drill bit. Make one hole in each corner of the rectangle to allow space for the jigsaw blade to cut out the frame.

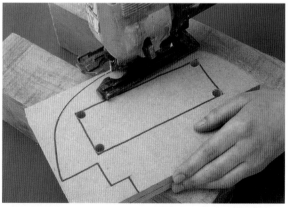

3 Carefully cut around the pencil outline on the MDF, using the jigsaw, to cut out the boat shape.

4 Insert the jigsaw blade into one of the drill holes and cut out the centre rectangle for the back of the frame.

5 On a third piece of MDF mark out the hull of the boat and the three portholes. First drill a hole and then use the jigsaw to cut out the shape.

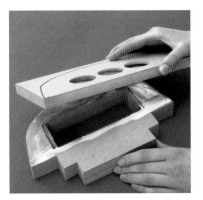

6 Glue the front of the boat with the three holes to the back of the boat. Let dry under a heavy weight.

7 Cut around the edge of the frame front and then smooth off the whole shape, using a surform and fine sandpaper.

8 When everything is sanded smooth, prime the boat with a coat of white acrylic primer.

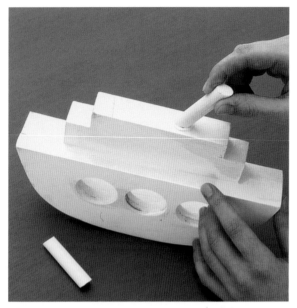

9 Cut out two funnels from wooden dowel. Cut them at a 60° angle and coat them with white acrylic primer. Glue them to the top of the boat.

10 Paint the boat with acrylic paints, using a medium paintbrush for the larger areas.

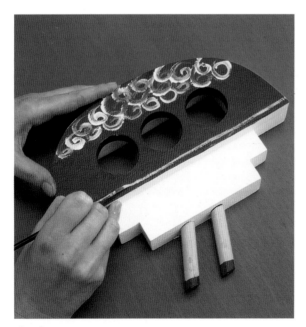

11 When the main colour has dried, paint the yellow plimsoll line and the white waves with a watercolour brush.

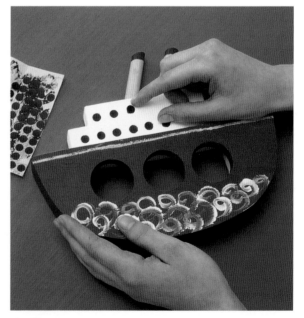

12 Paint over a sheet of white stickers with black acrylic paint. Let dry completely, then attach the stickers to the boat as small portholes.

MATERIALS

BRASS PICTURE WIRE (1) Essential for hanging up heavy frames.

BROWN PAPER TAPE (2) Tear the gummed tape into strips for natural-looking collage designs.

CANDLE (3) Use to create a distressed paint effect. Rub over the base coat paint before applying the top coat and lightly sanding.

CARDBOARD (4) There are many types of this cheap board available.

COLOURED PAPERS (5) Available in a wide range of shades.

COPPER NAILS (6) Use for decoration rather than strength.

COTTON STRING (7) Available in reels, string makes a good cheap decorating material.

DECOUPAGE PAPER (8) Copyright-free books are available that contain images to be photocopied for use in decoupage (see Suppliers).

HINGES (9) Use ornate hinges to join three frames together to make a triptych. Use the cheaper plain hinges to attach a stand to the back of a frame.

MEDIUM-DENSITY FIBREBOARD (MDF) (10 – used as background) A composite wood that is useful for making basic frame shapes, ready for painting. Always wear a protective mask when cutting MDF to avoid breathing in the fine particles of sawdust.

MOSAIC TILES (11) Use the small tiles to cover frames or to make a colourful edging. Because they are small, mosaic tiles rarely need to be cut to size.

MOULDINGS (12) The examples shown here are barley twist, quarter, battening and square moulding. Use them on their own or arrange several together to make your own combinations. They are usually sold in 2.4 m/8 ft lengths.

MOUNTING BOARD (13) Used for making picture mounts. Mounting board has a paper surface, top and bottom, which is cut through at an angle to reveal a layer of good quality cream card.

PICTURE HOOKS (14) Specially designed hooks for hanging pictures on walls. Use two hooks for hanging a heavy frame.

PLASTIC LIDS (15) The lids of household cleaning product containers can be used to make colourful motifs or mini frames. Plastic containers and bottles, and the caps, have many uses as cheap decorative materials.

PICTURE RINGS (16) Screw to the back of frames to hang pictures, with or without picture wire.

RIBBON (17) Use to make woven borders and hanging loops.

TISSUE PAPER (18) This translucent paper is available in a range of colours and makes a useful decorative material.

WATERCOLOUR AND ACRYLIC PAINTS (19) Use these water-soluble paints for colouring and tinting the finished frame.

EQUIPMENT

BALL PEIN HAMMER (1) This has one end round and the other end flat. Use to nail together the basic frames and for creating decoration.

CAKE TIN (PAN) (2) Individual tins make ideal moulds for papier-mâché or plasterwork.

90° CORNER CLAMPS (3) Use in pairs to hold the frame together when gluing.

CRAFT KNIFE & SCALPEL (4) A sharp knife is essential for many jobs. Use with a cutting mat to protect your work surface, and with a metal ruler for straight edges when cutting. Replace the blade as soon as it blunts.

CUTTING MAT (5) A self-healing mat that protects your work surface when using sharp knives. It allows you to make accurate cuts without the blade slipping.

ELECTRIC DRILL (6) An electric drill or hand drill is necessary for drilling holes when using a jigsaw blade, and to make holes for a dowel.

GLUE GUN (7) This provides a quick-drying glue that is useful for many of the projects.

ICE CUBE TRAY (8) A flexible tray commonly used in the home for making ice cubes. Fill it with plaster to create interesting shapes for decorating your frames.

JUNIOR HACKSAW (9) Use to cut hardboard and wooden moulding.

45° MAT CUTTER (10) Cuts cardboard at a 45° angle; gives a professional finish to the cut mount.

METAL RULER (11) Use for accurate measuring and as a guide when using a craft knife.

MITRE BLOCK (12) Pre-cut saw slots allow you to cut perfect 45° angle mitres.

PAINTBRUSHES (13) A standard 2 cm/¾ in household paintbrush is ideal for applying paint, glue or varnish. Use artists' brushes to apply fine detail. Always clean brushes thoroughly after use.

PAINT PALETTE (14) Mix your own colour combinations in a small palette to avoid wasting paint.

PAINT SCRAPER (15) Use a ridged scraper to create paint effects and to fold sheet metal over frames.

SCISSORS (16) A good, general pair of scissors is essential. Use small, sharp scissors for cutting out decoupage images.

SURFORM (17) Available from hardware stores in various sizes, it makes short work of filing down wood.

TENON SAW (18) Use this saw in conjunction with a mitre block to ensure accurate corners when cutting pieces of wood.

TIN SNIPS (19) Heavy duty shears for cutting tin sheets.

WOOD CHISEL (20) This wooden-handled tool is used for shaping and smoothing wood. Keep the end sharp, and protect it with a plastic cover when not in use.

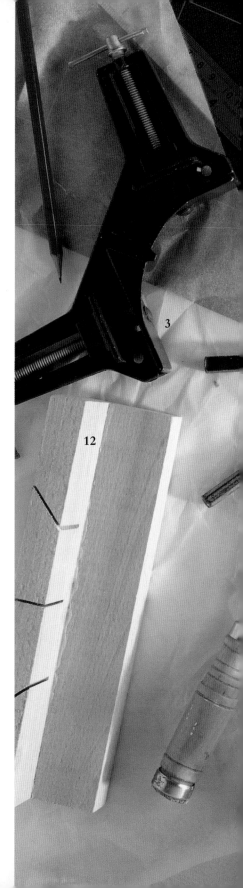

BASIC TECHNIQUES

The techniques for framing will vary according to the type of frame and the style of decoration, but some useful tips for specific techniques are given below. The most important things to get right are accuracy when cutting, and neatness, as these affect how the finished frame will look.

YOU WILL NEED

picture frame moulding
mounting board
mitre block & tenon saw
wood glue
2 corner clamps
hammer
corrugated fasteners
45° mat cutter
scalpel & metal ruler & cutting mat
masking tape
3 mm/¼ in picture glass
hardboard
junior hacksaw
panel pins (tacks)
brown paper tape
picture clips
small brass screws

MOUNTING AND FRAMING A PICTURE

1 When you have chosen your picture you need to choose a moulding to suit the subject. The moulding may be big and bold or small and delicate, modern or traditional. You can buy ready-decorated mouldings or add your own paint effect or finish.

2 Next, choose the mount for your picture. The type of mount is just as important as the frame, not only in the choice of colour and the width of the mount but also how close to the image it is placed.

3 To cut the picture moulding to length, use a mitre block and a tenon saw. This allows you to achieve accurate 45° angles. Remember to measure the frame from the inside edge and allow for the extra wood needed to take the 45° mitre cut.

4 Glue two pairs of corners at a time with wood glue and place in corner clamps so that you have a good strong seam that needs no filling later. Allow the glue to dry completely.

5 To add strength to the frame, hammer in a corrugated fastener in each corner. Make sure that the fasteners are hammered straight down.

6 Cut the mount cardboard with a 45° mat cutter. This gives a good, clean angle and a professional look to the mount. Working on the back of the mount, score the line first with a blade using a metal ruler as a guide. Gradually lower the blade and slice through the cardboard. To achieve good, crisp corners slightly over-cut each side so that the middle of the cardboard just drops out. Tape the picture to the mount with masking tape.

7 When you have all the main ingredients for the frame you can start to assemble it. With the frame face down, lower in the 3 mm/¼ in picture glass – this is thinner than window glass. It is readily available and can be cut to size by a glazier so that it sits in the rebate of the frame. The mount and picture are added next.

8 Next, use a junior hacksaw to cut a piece of hardboard to fit inside the rebate. Secure the hardboard in place with panel pins (tacks).

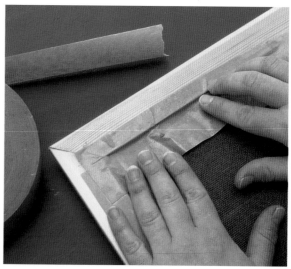

9 To seal the frame and prevent any dust getting in, cover the seam between the frame and the hardboard with brown paper tape. Let dry thoroughly.

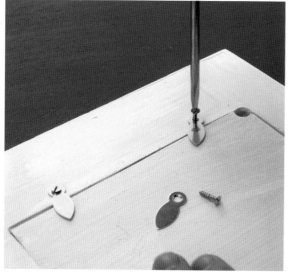

10 If you are likely to want to change the picture frequently, use brass picture clips that swivel. Attach them to the frame with small brass screws.

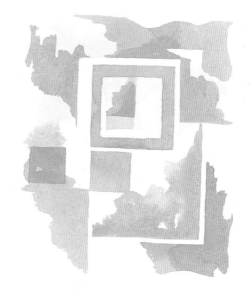

MAKING PICTURE STANDS

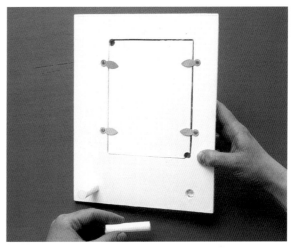

1 Make a hardboard stand and paint it to match the frame. Glue it to the back of the frame with a hinge so that it can also lie flat.

2 Alternatively, drill two holes into the back of the picture frame and insert a short length of wooden dowel.

HANGING PICTURES

1 To hang a picture, screw a ring screw into either side of the frame and securely tie on brass picture wire, to hang up the frame.

2 To hold the frame flush against a wall, use mirror plates. Screw them into the back of the frame and then slot them over screws in the wall. They are a strong and secure way of hanging a picture and you can paint the brass the same colour as the wall.

RESTORING A FRAME

1 Remove any old paint with paint stripper. Follow the manufacturer's instructions and neutralize the paint stripper before continuing.

2 Remove the last traces of paint with white spirit or turpentine, wire (steel) wool and sandpaper.

3 Next, prime the frame with a coat of acrylic primer, to provide a surface key in preparation for painting or gilding the frame.

4 Alternatively, leave the wood natural and enhance its beauty with wax or varnish. Here, liming wax is applied with wire (steel) wool to emphasize the natural grain of the wood.

TEMPLATES

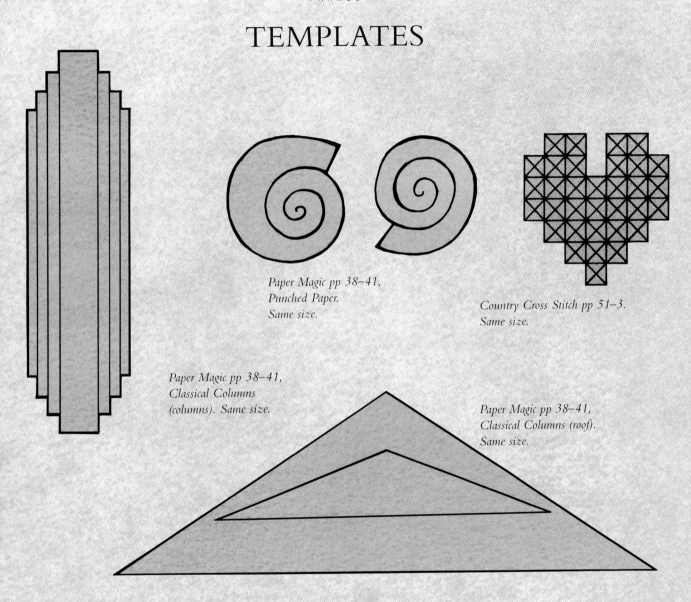

*Paper Magic pp 38–41,
Punched Paper.
Same size.*

*Country Cross Stitch pp 51–3.
Same size.*

*Paper Magic pp 38–41,
Classical Columns
(columns). Same size.*

*Paper Magic pp 38–41,
Classical Columns (roof).
Same size.*

Paper Magic pp 38–41, Classical Columns (steps). Same size.

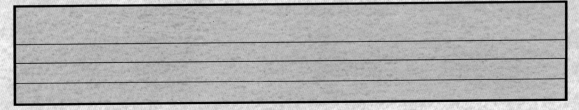

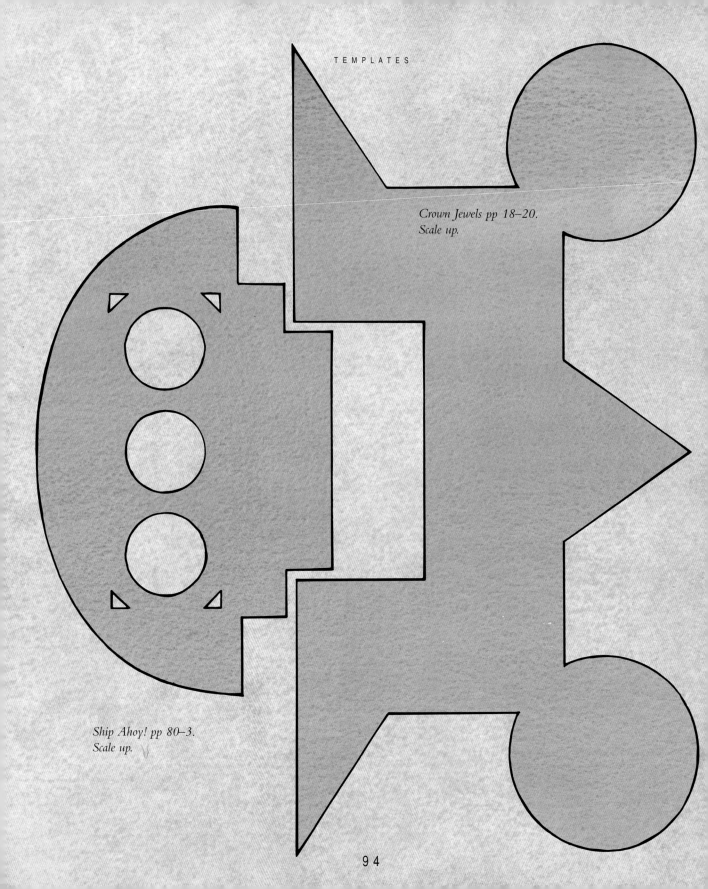

Crown Jewels pp 18–20.
Scale up.

Ship Ahoy! pp 80–3.
Scale up.

SUPPLIERS

The speciality materials and equipment that you will require for the projects in this book are available at any good art shop.

UNITED KINGDOM
Alec Tiranti Ltd
70 High Street
Theale
Reading RG7 5AR
Tel: (01734) 302 775

E. Ploton Ltd
273 Archway Road
London N6 5AA
Tel: (0181) 348 2838

Europacrafts
Hawthorn Avenue
Hull HU3 5JZ
Tel: (01482) 223 399

John Mylans Ltd
80 Norwood High Street
London SE27 9NW
Tel: (0181) 670 9161

UNITED STATES
Art Essentials of New York Ltd
3 Cross Street
Suffern NY 10901
Tel: (800) 283 5323

Createx Colors
14 Airport Park Road
East Granby CT 06026
Tel: (860) 653 5505

Dick Blick
P. O. Box 1267
Galesburg IL 61402
Tel: (309) 343 6181

Hofcraft
P. O. Box 72
Grand Haven MI 49417
Tel: (800) 828 0359

CANADA
Abbey Arts & Crafts
4118 East Hastings Street
Vancouver BC
Tel: 299 5201

Lewiscraft
2300 Yonge Street
Toronto
Ontario M4P 1E4
Tel: 483 2783

AUSTRALIA
Hobby Co
402 Gallery Level
197 Pitt Street
Sydney
Tel: (02) 221 0666

Spotlight (60 stores throughout)
Tel: freecall 1800 500021

ACKNOWLEDGEMENTS

The publishers would like to thank the following people: Ofer Acoo for the Sunflower Mirror, pp. 68–71; Victoria Brown for the Special Effects, pp. 8–11, Plaster Cast, pp. 15–17, Crown Jewels, pp. 18–20, Drift Away, pp. 21–3, Shell Frames, pp. 24–6, String Spirals, pp. 27–9, Made to Measure, pp. 34–7, Paper Magic, pp. 38–41, On the Tiles, pp. 42–4, Cut Flowers, pp. 45–7, Country Cross Stitch, pp. 51–3, Ribbon Weave, pp. 54–6, Sweet Hearts, pp. 57–9, Natural Selection, pp. 60–3, On Display, pp. 64–7, Plastic Fantastic, pp. 72–4, Fun Felt, pp. 75–7, Ship Ahoy!, pp. 80–3; Michael Savage for the Punched Tin, pp. 30–3, Metal Work, pp. 78–9; Karen Spurgin for Sequins and Beads, pp. 48–50; Liz Wagstaff for Good as Gold, pp. 12–14.

INDEX

acrylic paints, 84

backings, making, 90
basic techniques, 88–92

cake tins (pans), using, 57, 86
candles, 84
cardboard, 84
chisels, wood, 86
copper nails, 84
corner clamps, 86, 89
country cross stitch, 51–3
craft knives, 86
crown jewels, 18–20
cut flowers, 45–7
cutting mats, 86

decoupage, 45–6, 84
drift away, 21–3
drills, electric, 86

equipment, 86–7

fun felt, 75–7

gilding, 13–14, 92
  with spray paint, 26
glue guns, 86
gluing frames, 89
gold leaf, applying, 13–14
good as gold, 12–14

hacksaws, 86
hammer, ball pein, 86
hanging pictures, 91
hinged frames, 84
hooks, picture, 84

made to measure, 34–7
mat cutters, 86, 89
materials, 84–5
medium-density fibreboard
  (MDF), 84
metal rulers, 86
metal work, 78–9
mirror frames, 43–4, 68–70, 75–6
mirror plates, using, 91
mitre blocks, 86, 88
mosaic tiles, 43–4, 84
mouldings, 84
  combining, 34–6
  cutting and gluing, 88–9
mounts, cutting, 84, 86, 89

natural selection, 60–3

on display, 64–7
on the tiles, 42–4

paint, removing, 92
paintbrushes, 86
paint effects
  chequered effect, 8
  distressed effect, 8, 10, 84
  stamped effect, 8, 9
paint palettes, 86
paint scrapers, 86
paper magic, 38–41
papier-mâché, 19–20
plaster cast, 15–17
plastic fantastic, 72–4
plastic lids, 73, 84

punched tin, 30–3

restoring frames, 92
ribbon, 84
  ribbon weave, 54–6
ring screws, picture, 84, 91

scalpel, 86
scissors, 86
sequins and beads, 48–50
shell frames, 24–6
ship ahoy!, 80–3
special effects, 8–11
stands, making, 91
string, 84
  decorating with, 27–8
string spirals, 27–9
sunflower mirror, 68–71
suppliers, 95
surforms, 86
sweet hearts, 57–9

tape, brown paper, 84
templates, 93–4
tenon saws, 86
tiles, mosaic, 84
tin snips, 86
tissue paper, 84

watercolour paints, 84
wax, applying, 92
wire, brass picture, 84, 91